A POET'S DAY

Stephen Brooke

Eggshell Boats
2020

A POET'S DAY
©2020 Stephen Brooke and the Arachis Press

I will sit,
inside,
watching you pass,
outside,
the rest of this
poet's day.

All rights reserved. The text, art and design of this publication are the copyrighted work of Stephen Brooke and the Arachis Press and may not be reproduced nor transmitted in any form without the express written permission of the author or publisher, other than short quotes for review purposes.

ISBN 978-1-937745-70-7

Eggshell Boats is an imprint of the Arachis Press

Arachis Press
4803 Peanut Road
Graceville, FL 32440
http://arachispress.com

A Poet's Day

Chiaroscuro

Out on Peanut Road the trucks are rolling,
rumbling, basso continuo in the dark.

Dawn is half an hour away and the dogs
are eager for me to fill their bowls. They hear

the musics of the morning, mist-diffused,
rise from these fields, dewed webs of night time humming,

pulsing, pianissimo in tremulous
resonance, in tensions of light and dark.

The sun will sing its way into the day
as every voice of dawn joins in the chorus,

cardinal and mocking bird take up
the tune, rising, rising, on the stillness

to skies of promise. I am hidden here,
in chiaroscuro of my own hand,

the semblance of a man rapt in his shadows.
Fog and trees obscure the light of headlamps;

soon, those who hurry to a job somewhere
will be on the road, and tractors making

their way to fields of cotton or of peanuts.
Whether they spread poison or fertilizer

this day, I do not know. Sometimes both
at once, life and death together sprayed

up and down the rows, the farmer a god
handing out salvation and damnation

to those below his wheels. When the sun
has burnt away the mist, where shall we hide?

Out on Peanut Road, the traffic murmurs
of morning. There is coffee in the kitchen.

Cat on the Threshold

Uncertainty of gray, you hover half-in, half-out,
fearful of the trap, of no-way-out,

but eager to explore each mysterious corner,
each furniture cave and ledge.

Curiosity never killed in this house,
though it's been known to get one shooed.

Serious

I am a very serious fellow,
I think deep thoughts all day,
About why things are as they are
And if they'll stay that way.

But when I try to write them down,
Each nuanced contemplation,
I end up with these same cliches —
I end in desperation!

I've had no luck when I have tried
To write insightful verse,
And should I chance to fall in love,
It goes from bad to worse.

Not eloquent nor elegant
Nor even very witty,
My poems are not me at all —
It truly is a pity.

But I remain a serious fellow,
As serious as can be,
So here's another bunch of words
Arrayed as poetry.

Rise and Shine

Have I let my life sleep late,
lost the day that might have been,
grown too weary, grown too wary,
to go through it all again?

No, I'll toss my covers back,
shake my sleepy head and yawn,
rise once more to the occasion,
rise once more to greet the dawn.

Golden

This golden morning
whispers rain
through the trees,

a distance of squirrels
chasing the sun.

A Quest!

Name me a task, set me on the way
to my Holy Grail—
Through the night-dark forest to journey,
across the broad sea to sail,
and over the sky-kissed mountains to pass,
where the lost winds wail.
Name me a quest, set me a task—
one you know I shall fail.

A quest! A quest!

Give me a quest, show me a path,
tell what I must seek
along the roads beyond these roads
where I have proven weak—
these roads where we have walked and spoken
and found no more to speak.
Set me a path, give me a task—
let the way be bleak.

A quest! A quest!

Name me a task, grant me my quest,
send me where you will;
I sought elusive yesterdays—
the Grail lies distant still.
As distant as the morning sky
above the nearest hill—
to glimpse, to aspire, to name a quest
I never need fulfill.

The Kettle Calls

The kettle calls, insistently,
incessantly, saying *Do
you want that cup of tea or don't
you?* It's not a cheerful kettle.

It whistles no happy tune, no bird-like
song to brighten my morning. Only
that one shrill note until I pour
out its eager, boisterous contents.

But I, far too prone to wander
and wool-gather, need a loud
reminder that the water is
a-boil and that time, even breakfast

time, waits for no man. Not even
for distracted poets, seeking
words to finish one last line.
The kettle calls —

He Who Counts

The leper counts his fingers and his toes,
each morning's inventory. He is whole
today; tomorrow will be as it goes.
There comes a reckoning in time, a toll,
and what choice has he but to pay? None throws
the dice when naught remains except his soul.
In morning's gloom the leper counts and knows
he's but a prisoner on his parole.

Have I not counted so the passing days?
They vanished in the darkness, as the dreams
I can recall no longer. Nothing stays;
all falls away, away, until it seems
we are no longer. I who counts and knows
has seen that naught remains except his soul.

Name

I name myself 'poet.' It is
as good as any other word,
even one a poet might use.

Another might say 'bad poet.'
Qualifiers will be forgotten,
in time. People will murmur,

'He was a poet, you know,
years ago' and 'I wonder
if anyone reads him now.'

But I'll have the name.

Anything I Say

Never believe anything I say.
All the more, if it is
in a poem. I become
enamored of words, let them lead me

where they will. They put themselves
in my mouth. Even I
sometimes believe. Even I
can be seduced by the meaningless

phrase that sounds *just right*
and maybe it is. I'll not argue
the point with myself; I can't claim
to understand anything I say.

Bells

Yesterday is only two blocks
over. If we would cut through the neighbor's
back yard we might reach it before
it disappears. Hear its fading
ice-cream truck bells? They play
'Pop Goes the Weasel' over and over.

We have waited along our own streets
of green summer, listening
for each disappointment. You and I,
listing the flavors for each other,
counting our change — surely, time
must pass by and take what we offered.

Run, before it turns at the next corner.
Two blocks over; I am sure I heard
it there, ringing each lost promise
into twilight's mauve blanket. Later, our mothers
may scold us for spoiling our appetite,
but we know tomorrow shall never be as sweet.

Art School Girls

Art school girls were much too
full of themselves and the discovery
of their talents to be
introspective. Brash, ready

to hurt without thinking,
to throw themselves at their canvases
in crimson and ultramarine,
they spoke loudly to hear

themselves over their own chaos.
Everything broken could be put
back together and this week's
theories debated with this week's

boyfriend. How could I resist?
I who pondered each brush stroke,
each word, who knew the fragility
of what talent I had — I was

not for such nor they for me.

Vanilla

What flavors do you have?
Yesterday was vanilla
and so was most of last week;
isn't there something else
back there? Look in the bottom
of the freezer for me.
Any tooty-fruity or mocha?
No, no, not rocky road —
the way is hard enough
as it is. I'd rather
have another serving
of plain vanilla now.

Floats

Root beer floats are *de rigueur*
at the folk festival,
although I prefer a Coke
over my ice cream, usually.

Oh, yes, it will hit that proverbial
spot, halfway between
the Seminole camp and the Suwannee.
That's a long walk,

on a Memorial Day weekend,
a long hot walk toward Summer
and the music of fireflies
in the Florida twilight.

I've walked it more than once
or twice, a lover at my side;
the lovers have walked on
but not the remembering.

Kind Words

Have you spoken kindly of me
to those who followed after?
Or has my name become
a private joke, shared with your lovers,

snickering over a glass of wine?
It should be, for I was
a fool to let you go.
I hope your words are kind,

your memories may hold at least
some little fondness for
he whom you once loved.
He who loves you asks no more.

A Narrative

As you slip into my past, you become
a character in a book, someone I read
about, long ago. I have built
a narrative around you, remembering
those words, that look, discarding
the random parts that no longer
hold meaning. Could I have written you,
in idle moments? Are you the print
yet on my pages, the changeless black and white
I chose? I read, from time to time,
and know it is only a story, and that
perhaps some day I shall get
around to crafting the happy ending.

For You

Here's one more paint-by-numbers poem
meant to please everyone
but me. I'll mention colors
and women and the smell of roses.
I'll spread the sky with silent
stars and satin sheets.

What, you want more?
Come on down to the coffeehouse
every other Monday. I'll toss
my hair back and wear my best
poet's voice. You'll know
I'm reading for you. Only you.

Be a Hero

There is this part of me
that thinks I should be a hero,

that thinks I can be a hero
if I try hard enough.

And so I try, but never
hard enough to fly.

Loose Change

All the loose change
of my life is left
in a jar on the dresser
and never counted.

Each purchase, each time
I thought I needed
this, or thought *that*
would make me happy,

gives me another handful
of coins to add, to clink
one by one against
all I had hoped forgotten.

Out-Patient Surgery

The nurse is cute, in her green scrubs
and Sponge Bob clogs. What's her name?
Oh, I see. Lisa. It's on
her tag. No ring, either,

but I'm not here to chat up
girls, especially busy nurses
from surgery. Today, it is you
who needs their attention.

They wheel you off and I wait,
bored. So I write this poem
and wonder whether I should ask
Lisa for her number. Nah,

I guess not. And now it's time
to take you home, anyway.

Found

I have watched death's slow advance,
watched it overtake you day
by day, for these three years. Three
since you fell; now only by
the strength of my own arms do you rise,
only by my hand do you
eat, drink, live. None of it
do I begrudge, though I may
at times, grow weary, though I may
recall the pain of once, of failing
to be the one you expected, feeling
myself the least loved. Is that why
I am with you now? No matter.
I seek nothing from you, you who
no longer know me. I seek nothing
from myself. Nothing that
I have not already found.

Gloves

For your amusement, I made balloon
animals of the surgical gloves.
There was a supply, bedside,
ready to the nurses' steady,
sturdy hands. I milked that cow,
made that rooster crow, diverted

you but Styx sticks to its course.
Carried further toward the dark
of whatever Hades held for you
in his own dexterous hands, were you
reaching toward them even as I
transformed latex and kept my watch?

Was it for my amusement, I made
balloon animals as you took
the long way around to death?
Divert me. Let me laugh at my own
corny jokes and never notice
that river, that stick of licorice

that twists away and back again
for each of us. I only twisted
gloves, inflated with my living
breath and tied so it would not
escape, to give some brief existence
to balloon animals. For your amusement.

Un Aeroplane

One day, she no longer
understood the piano
but sat staring at the keys,
Satie's *Sports et Divertissements*
open before her.
All the hours, forgotten,
all the times her hands
had followed the sarcastic
notes. *Teins! un aeroplane…*
Look up, look up,
before you also
forget me.

Mother

I have not yet
had to say goodbye
to my mother

a little more of her
leaves each day

A Poet's Day

A British-ism: "having a poet's day" means leaving work at noon and spending the rest of the day drinking in a pub.

Outside,
the sun is poised
at the top of its arc,
the better to watch
workers hurrying
to their lunches,
the break in their everyday.

Inside,
I've been at my desk
since dawn,
coffee and words
poured together
until I'm too full
to hold any more.

Outside,
down a few streets
and over a few more,
is a place, where,
inside,
is a cool corner,
dim-lit by a curved
glass window,

and I will sit,
inside,
watching you pass,
outside,
the rest of this
poet's day.

Cracks

If I use bits of you
to fill the cracks in me
is that so wrong?

These days the wind
blows right through me.

I shall make up for it
by telling you lies
disguised as sweet love songs

and you may pretend
to believe each one,

though they are but that wind,
blowing, blowing,
through the cracks.

Airports

I do not know airports.
Other people hurry through them,
one scene in a novel
or TV show or life.

They catch a plane. They catch
a taxi to home or to hotel.
I don't know taxis either.
They are a foreign country.

I never sat in their back seats,
looking out at a city.
I have never flown over a city;
I have no business there.

I do not know your lives,
you who hurry from place
to place, you with your luggage.
I do not know airports.

The Stoa

I studied many schools
of philosophic thought;
I listened to the words
those wiser than I taught.
But in the end I chose
to follow the Stoic way,
for we just sit on the porch
and pass the time of day.

Zeno likes to whittle,
Chrysippus sleeps the day long;
Aurelius pulls out his banjo
and sometimes gives us a song.
It sure beats the Academy,
or sleeping with the dogs;
we leave that to Diogenes
(as well as wearing no togs).

We come up with aphorisms,
when we don't talk about the weather,
like 'anger is an obstruction'
or 'we're meant to work together.'
But a porch is for relaxing
so we settle back in our chairs,
philosophize on our stoa
and forget our cares.

The Critic

As I drifted down the muddy stream
of consciousness, a Nihil Crocodile
surfaced by my flimsy boat of dream
and, asking me if we might talk a while,
pontificated, shedding bogus tears,
on books and music and the latest style.
Ad nauseam, he criticized his peers;
we floated on, mile after murky mile.

"I admit to hating all things new;
it is my job," he told me, "as a critic.
Though truly, I dislike the old stuff, too —
so I don't bother being analytic."
He dove then, stating as if well-intentioned,
"I hope my words have proven catalytic."
But had he smaller teeth I would have mentioned
he came off as no more than parasitic.

Girl Writes Poetry

She showed me her work:
twice as many poems
as I have written
in twice as many years.
One or two, I liked.

Afloat

   Others swim laps in the pool of self-pity
until they can no longer find any reason
to stay above water, remain afloat, live.

   Yet I continue this, my narrative;
denying pain, ever I seek to be witty.
I watch, I survive, for a day, for a season.

   Each word I write may be read as fresh treason,
or spurned as no more than a meaningless ditty;
tomorrow was not mine to take nor to give.

Fair Fight

Some days, I believe life isn't fair.
Others, I suspect that I deserve
all the crap it hands me. Either way,

I'll never be that guy who says 'life isn't
fair, deal with it.' The guy who takes that crap
instead of taking a swing in hopes of landing

a fist to life's smug face. Not that life
will ever notice but I always feel
a hell of a lot better. Even if

the knockout punch is waiting in the next round.

Paper Champion

It's all quite well to be writer
but I'd rather be a fighter,
lay out opponents with my left hook
instead of sparring with a book.

I've tried to shuffle like Ali
but shuffling papers is it for me;
and though my jabs are with a pen,
I hope a punch lands now and then!

Ah, perhaps it's just as well
that I chose not to answer the bell;
an author deals with black and white
while one is black and blue, post-fight.

Punch

I've fallen again.
Let me lie here a moment

to catch my breath,
gather my wits.

Then I'll get up
and take another punch.

Secret Identity

I spent too many years
as Clark Kent. Now I
won't take off my cape,
can't stop flying. It's up,
up, and away all the time.

Someday, I'll fall from the sky.
Someday, when I'm no longer
faster than a speeding
bullet. But isn't that
the best way to go out?

To fall, fall, fall as fire,
a comet, an omen. To be,
when I've forgotten my own
secret identity.

Four Stupid Little Poems

Prices

I am here, each day,
selling myself to the world.
It's time I cut my prices
once again.

The Word

I sought *le mot juste*,
the right word, the needed word.
No one could understand
what it meant.

Awards

My awards and diplomas
have finally proven useful.
The backs are good for jotting
down grocery lists.

Girlfriend

I found the same drawback
with every girlfriend.
They wanted to go places
and do things.

STOP

I've been shown a sign
that the end is near:
red and with eight sides,
STOP written big and clear!
It's good to reach the end;
now all that I fear
is choosing left or right
and going on from here.

Day

One day, these days,
is very much like
another. Sunday
or Tuesday has
the same sunrise,
the same routines
and need-to-be-dones.
And they do
need to be done,
oh yes. Today,
tomorrow, next week.
I'll be there; just
don't ask me what
day it is.

Always

If I found one
of my old love songs
and changed her name
to yours, would you
know the difference?
Would you believe
I sang only
for you? I would.
I always believe.

I Am the Blues

I am the blues the wind sings to the trees,
The lonely distant sigh borne on the breeze
That calls the broken heart across the night.
Caressing misted strings of pale moonlight,
A moaning slide guitar built of regret,
I speak the names of loves they can't forget.

Knowing the Blues

Maybe you don't know
what the blues can do;
maybe you don't know
how they fill your soul
with the cold, cold night.

If I sing the blues,
give me Billie's voice —
the night was in her soul,
oh yes, the darkest night
no neon could send packing.

No lover, no high can fill
a hole that deep, that empty.
No frantic empty hours
of dancing and drinking can warm
your desperate, deep-down chill.

You don't know the blues, kid,
haven't lived the blues.
Haven't heard the wind
sing them through the endless
hours of the night.

Filling Up

My glass is empty
and the bottle that filled it
and for all I know the whole
damned distillery may have
shut down, all those oak barrels
now tacky furniture
in someone's paneled den.
Were I a drinker,
one of those barfly poets,
I'd not be sitting here,
holding the empty past.
I'd be filling up,
anywhere I could, trying
to replace what runs out through
the cracks. But empty is empty
and I can live with that.
Yeah, I can live with that.

Rowboat

How did I end up in this rowboat
with Anne, heading for God?

Or is that the isle of Bali Hai,
there over the horizon's curve?

My heart's desire waits there,
I'm sure, unattainable

unless one knows the right people.
Won't you put in a good word for me?

After all, I've spent a lifetime
in search of your happiness,

knowing none myself
save when I pull the hardest.

Less

Who could name the person
I yearned to become?
Add up all my past —
I'm less than the sum.

Nothing to be learned
from my deconstruction,
willing participant
in my own abduction,

making action movies
none will ever see,
setting off explosions
that maim only me.

Too late to be rescued
from the things I do;
let me drown again
trying to save you.

For it is the natural
state of all these things
to remain unnatural,
fly with stunted wings

in pursuit of nothing.
What's left to assess?
Add me up again —
I remain far less.

Onshore

The wind had come onshore
and we could peddle home,
breeze at our backs, the rain
following behind.

It swept us on, that breeze;
it whispered how the day
ever grows forgetful
of morning's every promise.

Out over swamp and prairie
built the towering dark
of distant afternoons —
remembered, now, remembered

in dream of slabs of storm,
summer's lightning licking
along our gray horizons.
Remembered, as a sun

that called us to the now
empty rain-swept beaches.
Our past has its own paths
through other afternoons;

it will not be found
along those ways, beneath
the palms that swayed so when
the wind had come onshore.

The Shadow of the Swell

When a younger man, a time forever gone,
I'd drive through the night, long hours to find dawn,
stand by the Atlantic as the sun would rise,
watch the crashing surf beneath peach-tinted skies.

My heart beat in rhythm to the ocean's song,
rising with each wave, far-journeyed yet still strong,
loud as thunder's drums and subtle as the mist
that clung to its crest, by morning's breezes kissed.

Once I sought truths in the shadow of the swell;
time's lost lambent song has held me in its spell.
Does the sea dance now on that remembered shore?
Shall I seek all that eluded me before?

I have journeyed long, to find and know this day,
whispering its secrets to the foam-flecked gray;
still I understand too little of the wind,
still it wordless murmurs of how I have sinned.

I live in the shadow that the swell once cast
when a younger man, a time forever past,
and each heartbeat is a wave upon the beach
I must yearn for through the night and never reach.

Among the Words

You ask me who I am but my answers
only confuse the both of us.

All my letters are too polite;
I am not found among the words.

Look for me in my poems;
that is where I tell the best lies.

Half-Full

I drank from the half-full glass
until it was empty, utterly
empty, and my asking
no longer refilled it.

No, not half-way, not even
a quarter — whatever pitcher
held our future had been carried
to some other table

where some other couple
drank deeply and thanked
a tired waitress.

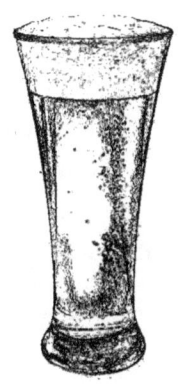

Ignore

Ignore your problems
long enough, they go away
or you do

and that's the same thing, right?
Let's pour another drink and wait.

A Noise

I have no lies,
I have no truths,
only words that might
mean something to someone.

They hold nothing,
nothing for me,
no meanings, no subtle truths,
no, not even lies.

Let me craft some
into a noise
for you, a nonsense song,
a drone to mask the traffic,

that endless passing
toward tomorrow.
Don't look out the window;
nothing's to be seen.

Inverted

The role of the poet
is to describe the world
while standing on his head.

Who will recognize
her own house
from these upside-down

words? Will birds
alight in such
a garden? I've inverted

my world and now
is somehow past
and you write poems of me,

as the coins
slip from my pockets
and into the empty sky.

An Existentialist Lullaby

Hush little baby, don't say a word,
For existence is absurd.
Free will is a curse, you see,
There's no point to what may be.

But if you should choose to choose,
Let what happens but amuse;
Nothing can be blamed on fate —
Meaning is what we create.

Every looking glass is cracked —
all that we can do is act;
So, hush little baby, don't say a word,
For existence is absurd.

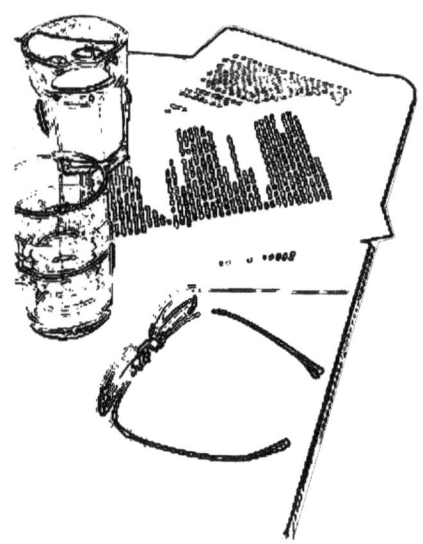

Jabber

I, the jabbering ape, have sought
the secrets of life so I might fling
them at my brethren. We will howl
at the universe from our trees.

Every storm holds voices we can not
understand. The eyes of the sky
tell of its great hunger, its roaring
holds the memory of ages

lost in our abyss. Jabber,
brother! Howl, sister! Even
time must hear us before it ends.
Even God will understand.

Bird

Who caught the bird
that flies upside-down?
Give it to the king
to place in his crown.
Each wink to the wise,
each wink to a clown,
laughs at the lies
I've told this town.

Here is the word
I bought at your store.
It will not sing.
It cries for more.
My morning star
knocks at the door
but the window's ajar
for her encore.

You preferred
a different word?
You preferred
one never heard?
Don't be absurd —
I've caught your bird.

Now

There is no now,
no present, only
a line between
past and future,

a knife edge cleaving
what was from what
will be. Who can
live there, stand

on such a blade?
We may divide
then from then.
We may say *that*

is in the past.
Was that not *we*?
Will it not be
we tomorrow?

It remains
one life, our life,
and in the end,
at the end,

there is no now.

The Woman in the Other Room

Knowing you are there
is all that's needed,
that our lives will

cross and intertwine
here and there,
now and then,

that we are two vines
climbing together
toward whatever heaven

we might dream
but rooted in
our common soil.

You are the woman
in the other room,
making your way

as I make mine,
through the wordless days
of this house

and of our lives.
The quiet of you,
the knowing you are there

and I am here,
becomes all —
all that is needed.

Order

I put these words in place
so they might speak their lines
but, alas, discover
they have their own minds.
Allusion proves elusive
and my meanings stray—
One may order language
but it does not obey.

Rooted

My words are rooted in me;
they take some of my soil,

some of my soul, when I
transplant them to the page.

Be careful. You wouldn't want
to get your hands dirty.

Hobble

It is no wonder that my verses hobble—
I've placed the accents on the wrong syllable.
And it is true my lines but seldom scan—
with extra feet, they've often tripped before they ran.

Indeed, my poems do not move in quite
the meters many might insist are 'right'
and scattered through the iambs you will see
a dactyl, or two of them, and perhaps even three.

Yet, still I'm told I have a certain way
with triteness, boring language, and cliche,
so hobble on I shall in clumsy verse—
for many do unwittingly write worse.

Believable

What I don't know
I am quite able
to make up.

Will practice make me
believable?

Safekeeping

I'm one of those people
who wants to put forever
in his pocket,
carry it home
and keep it safe.
But I always forget
it's in there, crumpled,
and worn, lint-covered,
until I throw it away
with the used Kleenex
and sticky cough-drops
and business cards
that can't be read
anymore.

Impractical

I am enough of an impractical dreamer
to mistrust impractical dreamers.
Let them write their books and paint their paintings.
Let them sing love songs

but don't believe the words.
They'll sing them to another next week.
Don't ask them to lead
nor hire them to follow.

They'll take their own way,
not suffering those they see as fools.
Listen to them, yes; learn to see
the things that they have seen

but mistrust the impractical dreamers.
Mistrust me.

Small

I write the small sins of my life
very large. I fill books with them,
dressed up as great passions, the vices
of a man that I am not.

Let me lie to you. Let me
hide in a thicket of words, grown
tall as jungles, dense as morning's
sunlit distances. Time will

remember only these pages, singing
their tunes across tomorrow, singing
of this small man, written large.

Inertia

I had a television that only worked
when I turned it on its side so I spent
a year watching it while lying on *my* side
until it finally stopped working at all.

Maybe I'm cheap or maybe I just let
inertia have its way. Not that inertia
has a way; it just sits there, right?
Sometimes I've just sat there, too, waiting

for life to chew me up and spit out
the bones. But that gets boring, after
a while, as boring as lying on my side
in bed to watch a broken television.

Easier

You know it.
The world knows it.
It's easier to draw back
than to reach out,
easier not to take the chance,
not to risk our comfortable pain.

It's easier to live empty,
to hold that pain to our hearts
each day, until it becomes
who we are,

and who we are
becomes
nobody.

Sidekick

Every hero needs a sidekick;
I'll let you be mine.
It's not a demanding position,
I'm sure you'll do just fine.
I'll ask for your advice,
but follow my own design,
and, of course, I'll get the girl;
you'll console yourself with wine.

You'll share in my derring-do,
yes, each and every deed;
and be seen as an hero too,
although of a lesser breed.
My horse will be tall and fiery,
a truly worthy steed;
you'll ride a little behind me —
a donkey is all you'll need.

And when you take that bullet
that was aimed at my breast,
I shall surely grieve,
tell all you were the best.
But I must find another
to laugh at my every jest;
for a hero needs a sidekick
to share in his quest.

Hide

Love poems hide along the road.
They wait for you or maybe for
the next who passes. Not for me.
They hide and hidden remain and I

do not bother to look any more.
Once, the poems darted out
into traffic, barking. They
did not know that I would pay

them no attention. They did not know
that I would drive on, not caring
when they fell beneath my wheels.
Now, the poems have learned, and hide.

They hide along the road, and wait.

Novel

The latest novel from the poet
appeared today. Who will remember
his verses? The words are so few,
when held up for comparison.

Or will some future reader, looking
up from the page, tell her companion,
'He also wrote fiction, I understand,
but it wasn't very good.'

New Mask

The mask comes off and nothing lies beneath;
the door is opened, one more empty room
pretends to be my life. A poet, now?

Each midnight line is gibberish, come morn;
each kiss becomes another sweet farewell
to rhyme with hell. Oh, well! Call me tomorrow

for I am done with being yesterday
and bought a brand new mask. It was on sale,
half-price, the third day after Halloween.

Stale

My words have gone stale.
I'll sell them now at half-price,
stack them on the day-old shelf.
Give them away to those

who can not afford
fresh-baked verses,
the still-steaming loaves
from the ovens of youth.

Make a pudding of my poems —
some sugar to sweeten,
a custard to moisten,
to fill the empty spaces.

That might make them palatable.
All goes stale, you know,
in time. That needn't keep
us from our just desserts.

Harvest

There is this weariness that comes,
whispers softly, once again,
lay down your burdens, take the leap
into darkness, into sleep,
perhaps to fly across the night,
perhaps to fall into the deep,
fall forever, or but end.

Ah, the Bard said all this better
than I might hope; the rub is there,
is it not? The price is steep
and as we sow, so shall we reap
or maybe not. This harvest fails
beneath the trampling of my feet.

Words

I can not but envy
clumsy, honest words,
the simplicity
I have never owned.

For my words all come
too readily: facile
verses, emptied of
the truths they might have held

before I made them mine.

Thrift Store

These dreams no longer fit.
I'll box them up, donate
them to the thrift store,
let them be fingered, held up
to see the size, the wear.
No one there will know who once
wore such impractical garments.

Matters

When everything matters,
nothing matters
or is it the other
way around?

Everything matters
the same, anyway,
and, every day,
life has the same point

or lack thereof.
It all means what
you will or won't
let it mean,

so be in love
with life one day
and hate it the next.
It matters or doesn't.

Trains

Word after word: toy trains of words
that go around and around
have carried me. Shall I wave
to the painted metal people

I created and placed just so?
Each fixed smile, each plastic facade,
becomes a landmark, reassurance
for the secret passenger,

the hobo who seeks empty boxcars.
I could sleep here forever, lulled
by the songs that I have woven
of a transformer's muted hum.

Word after word: the shiny stock
that should be bound for distant towns
encompasses my days' horizons;
I no longer count the passing.

Let Them

All of yesterday's
unfulfilled prophecies
turned up at my door.

Let them knock. Let them ring.

I'm not opening up.
Tomorrow's news has gone to bed
and I must do the same.

Let them cry, *remember me?*

Memory is such
a fragile box. It cracks, it leaks
its dark pools of denial.

Let them flow away, fading

into imagination's
desert lands. There they shall
become the drink of prophets.

My Pain

This is my pain.
I am greedy;
I will not share.
This is my pain
to hold like the last note
of a fading song.

Its emptiness
fills me, takes
away the breath
of everyday,
the ceaseless despair
of existence.

This is my pain:
meaningless,
mindless, a candle
left to burn
itself away
and cast no light.

Deposit

God returned my deposit,
canceled my reservation;
I'll find no lodging tonight

nor shall I dine upon
moon pie and frosted stars.
Shall we be homeless together,

dancers in the darkened
alleyways of time?
Wear the red dress for me

once more; dawn will open
its doors soon enough.
You shall shine like the sun

of my new morning.

Nets

From their crescent boats, the poets cast
their fathers' ancient and oft-mended nets
across the dark, into the deep, unknown,

unknowable, in hopes of tangling truth,
some blind supple swimming truth, in woven
words, a mesh of metaphor. Their fathers,

yes, their fathers' fathers cast them so,
catching their own meanings. Those decay
upon the silvered shores. The moon is setting.

Map

The map bequeathed me proved inaccurate,
 yet I found my way from there to here.

Who wandered with me all that way but you?
 We who lost our way but did not fear

have reached the well-marked road at last, come dusk.
 Walk with me into the night drawn near.

Tarnished

Each day, the blind man walks
his remembered path,
turning as he has ever

turned, pausing where he
paused before. Those stars
that guided him now move

in darkened mirrors, in nameless
constellations, lost
promises of night.

And all his mirrors sing
their tarnished prophecies
into a dream of dawn.

Sun

Laugh or cry, curse or pray,
the sun still sets at end of day.

What we do, what we say,
each memory is swept away.

Accept what is, question why,
no answer serves to satisfy.

Curse or pray, laugh or cry,
the sun sinks lower in your sky.

Triumph

Some days, my ambition
is to conquer the world.

Others, only to convince
myself to remain alive.

Tonight, I shall celebrate
the latest triumph.

Wordless

Time disappears into
the insistent rain
and now might be tomorrow
or an hour ago,

marked only by the clock
of opaque windows, the tick
of dripping eaves. I am
as formless as the gray

taste of this day, washed
clean and purposeless.
As the birds, I huddle
stilled, my song forgotten,

while the wordless rain
murmurs against the roof.
No shadows lie between
me and my horizons;

has storm darkened the fields
or does night come at last?
All answers lie in sleep
and the morning sun.

Together

We could go out by ourselves,
together. You sit across from me
and listen to your own conversation
while I enjoy my company.

It shouldn't be any more boring
than some dates you've been on, and lots
less stressful. Yes, let's go out
together and ignore each other.

And at the end, we might nod
a friendly farewell — parting will be
neither sweet nor sorrow. But it
will be separate checks, please.

We Say Nothing

Let me make mistakes with you,
leaving the regrets of tomorrow
to tomorrow. They will come.

To say nothing, beautifully,
says enough. The flame yet kisses
what we threw upon the hearth,

yet devours each hope. We only
mark our foreheads with the ashes
and go forth to sin no more.

We say nothing of tomorrow;
we say nothing, beautifully.

Changed

The sky, going home, was much like the sky
I saw, leaving. All else was changed.
Changed like a chameleon or like
the water at Cana? I could use

the wine of miracles right now.
I could get drunk upon it. The sky
may be drunken too, forgetting
its way home until tomorrow

morning. Then all things will be
as we remembered. Sleep on it.

Tempest

Tonight holds the promise of storm;
electric incense burns the breeze.

What voices murmur, basso, beyond
the distant footlights of my horizon?

It is an old song, this tune that flickers
in overture to the tempest.

Raindrops

I can not count the raindrops
but know they have a number;
they sang upon my rooftop
as I fell into slumber,
and each told me its name,
each whispered and was gone,
with all of night time's dreams
forgotten in the dawn.

Odds

I have seen the doors of destiny
open before me, seen the calm, cold stars
wink to life in the void. Hear their voices,

lifting songs that hold no key. Once I
learned such tunes, misunderstanding each
promise. Like that famous cat which is

alive and dead at once, these futures both
exist and don't. Did I choose? Ask
the angels and the stars. Ask those beguiled

by the lurid signs along their roads.
Signs and wonders, portents of my fate,
point ever away from here. I've heard the gossip

of the hard-faced women on this street.
All the night, they whisper to each other,
laying odds. Which regret will I

ask to wear when they have done their weaving?
Tonight I count the stars. Their number must
add up to something, something I might believe.

Good Night

I have struggled. We all
struggle and suffer and die
and it may or may not

mean a damned thing when
the universe turns out
the lights and says 'good night.'

This old mix of anger
and amusement sees me
through this day and the day

after and another.
Each only replaces the last,
as I have replaced myself,

year by year, cell
by cell, becoming an ever
poorer copy, till none

can read me. Then, turn out
the light. Turn it out
and we will say 'good night.'

Thank you for reading A POET'S DAY. I hope you have enjoyed this collection of my poems. ~ *Stephen Brooke*

Stephen Brooke is a poet, novelist, artist, and sometime surfer, residing in the Florida Panhandle.
http://stephenbrooke.com

Other poetry titles by Stephen Brooke,
all available from the Arachis Press:
  Pieces of the Moon
  Dreamwinds
  Retellings
  The Tower
  Fields of Summer
  Awful Alvin and Other Peculiar Poems (Juvenile)
  Voyages
  Magic

Eggshell Boats is an imprint of the Arachis Press
http://eggshellboats.com
http://arachispress.com

www.ingramcontent.com/pod-product-compliance
Lightning Source LLC
Chambersburg PA
CBHW051714040426
42446CB00008B/884